SIMPLE SCIENCE EXPERIMENTS
MATTER AND MATERIALS

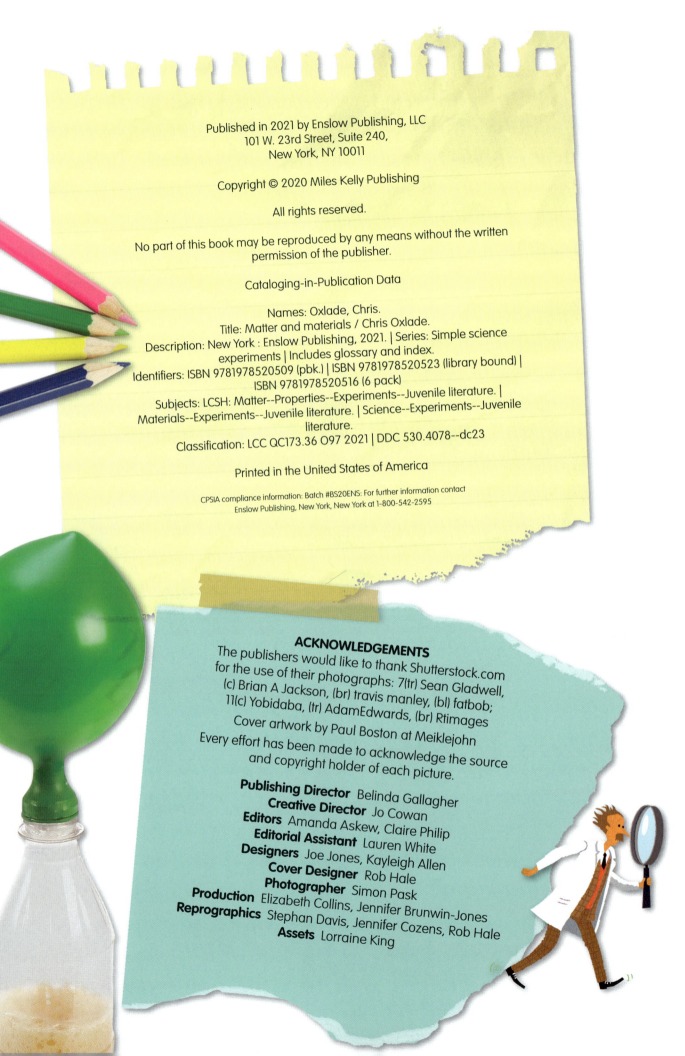

Published in 2021 by Enslow Publishing, LLC
101 W. 23rd Street, Suite 240,
New York, NY 10011

Copyright © 2020 Miles Kelly Publishing

All rights reserved.

No part of this book may be reproduced by any means without the written permission of the publisher.

Cataloging-in-Publication Data

Names: Oxlade, Chris.
Title: Matter and materials / Chris Oxlade.
Description: New York : Enslow Publishing, 2021. | Series: Simple science experiments | Includes glossary and index.
Identifiers: ISBN 9781978520509 (pbk.) | ISBN 9781978520523 (library bound) | ISBN 9781978520516 (6 pack)
Subjects: LCSH: Matter--Properties--Experiments--Juvenile literature. | Materials--Experiments--Juvenile literature. | Science--Experiments--Juvenile literature.
Classification: LCC QC173.36 O97 2021 | DDC 530.4078--dc23

Printed in the United States of America

CPSIA compliance information: Batch #BS20ENS: For further information contact Enslow Publishing, New York, New York at 1-800-542-2595

ACKNOWLEDGEMENTS
The publishers would like to thank Shutterstock.com for the use of their photographs: 7(tr) Sean Gladwell, (c) Brian A Jackson, (br) travis manley, (bl) fatbob; 11(c) Yobidaba, (tr) AdamEdwards, (br) Rtimages
Cover artwork by Paul Boston at Meiklejohn
Every effort has been made to acknowledge the source and copyright holder of each picture.

Publishing Director Belinda Gallagher
Creative Director Jo Cowan
Editors Amanda Askew, Claire Philip
Editorial Assistant Lauren White
Designers Joe Jones, Kayleigh Allen
Cover Designer Rob Hale
Photographer Simon Pask
Production Elizabeth Collins, Jennifer Brunwin-Jones
Reprographics Stephan Davis, Jennifer Cozens, Rob Hale
Assets Lorraine King

SIMPLE SCIENCE EXPERIMENTS

MATTER AND MATERIALS

Chris Oxlade
Consultant: John Farndon

CONTENTS

5 Notes for helpers
6 What is matter?
7 What are materials?
8 Using this book
10 Scientist kit

A material can be described by its properties, such as its color or strength.

Experiment time!

12 Ice to water to steam
14 Create crystals
16 Mixing like magic
18 Can you mix it?
20 Splitting the mix
22 Salty to freshwater
24 Color separation
26 Cabbage colors
28 Bubbles and froth
30 Electric bubble maker

32 Glossary and Index

What shape are salt crystals?
Find out on page 15.

Do oil and water mix?
Find out on page 18.

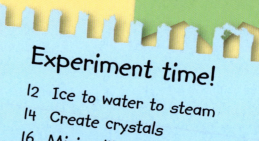

What does bleach do to colored water?
Find out on page 27.

Notes for HELPERS

Help and hazards

- All of the experiments are suitable for children to conduct, but they will need help and supervision with some. This is usually because the experiment requires the use of a stovetop or oven, a knife or scissors, or food coloring. These experiments are marked with a "Help needed" symbol.

- Read the instructions together before starting and help to assemble the equipment before supervising the experiment.

- It may be useful to carry out your own risk assessment to avoid any possible hazards before the child begins. Check that long hair and any loose clothing are tied back.

- Also check that materials such as bleach are disposed of safely, and that the oven or stovetop is turned off after use.

Extra experiments

You can also help children with the extra experiments in this book, or search the Internet for more similar ideas. There are hundreds of science experiment websites to choose from.

www.lovemyscience.com This website is packed with simple, fun experiments for children to enjoy.

www.sciencebob.com/experiments/index.php Engaging science experiments with clearly explained instructions will keep kids busy for hours.

www.sciencefun.org/kidszones/experiments You will find lots of entertaining and informative experiments on this colorful, interactive website.

Publisher's note to educators and parents: Our editors have carefully reviewed these websites to ensure that they are suitable for students. Many websites change frequently, however, and we cannot guarantee that a site's future contents will continue to meet our high standards of quality and educational value. Be advised that students should be closely supervised whenever they access the Internet.

What is MATTER?

Matter makes up everything you can see, from the water in your glass, to the chair you are sitting on. It also makes up some things you cannot see, such as the air you breathe. There are three states of matter, which make up nearly every substance in the universe.

The three states of matter

Everything around us is either a solid, liquid, or gas, made up of billions of units called atoms. Atoms are some of the smallest objects that exist, and are invisible. Two or more atoms joined together make up a molecule. Groups of molecules make up a substance.

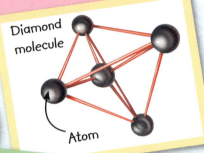
Diamond molecule
Atom

Changing state

A substance can change from one state to another by gaining or losing energy, in the form of heat.

Solid

Atoms or molecules in a solid cannot move. They are tightly packed together, so they keep their shape and feel firm.

Liquid

In a liquid, atoms or molecules can move or flow, but they stay the same distance apart. The links between the molecules are weaker than in a solid. A liquid can flow and fill the shape of its container.

Gas

Atoms or molecules in a gas move quickly and in all directions. The molecules bounce around because the forces between them are not strong enough to keep them together.

If a liquid is cooled, it turns into a solid. This is called freezing.

If a gas is cooled, it turns into a liquid. This is called condensing.

If a solid is heated, it turns into a liquid. This is called melting.

If a liquid is heated, it turns into a gas. This is called evaporation.

What are MATERIALS?

Every substance is made from a material, or a combination of materials. A material's properties, such as strength or flexibility (bendiness), make it useful for different things. Modern materials can be natural or synthetic (chemically man-made).

Natural resources

Since ancient times, a large number of everyday materials have been made from plants, such as cotton and wood. Natural materials such as these need to be recycled (made into new things) and reused, so they do not run out.

Wood

There are many different types of wood, varying in strength, color, and weight. Wood comes from trees and is mainly used for fuel, or in construction (building).

Chair

Rubber bands

Rubber

Natural rubber is made from milky sap, called latex, found in some tropical trees. However, it can also be made synthetically. Rubber is flexible, tough, and waterproof, which makes it useful for making car tires.

Synthetic substances

Plastic, steel, and glass are examples of synthetic materials. Sometimes a mixture of both natural and synthetic materials can be used – for example in clothing.

Drink bottle

Plastic

Waterproof, long-lasting, and strong, this synthetic material is mainly made from substances found in petroleum (crude oil). Plastics can be easily shaped and molded and thus are used in many everyday products.

Rope

Polyester

This synthetic material is often used to make clothing, as it dries quickly and holds its shape well. Rope is also often made from polyester because it is very strong.

7

USING this book

Each experiment has numbered instructions and clear explanations about your findings. Read through all the instructions before you start an experiment, and then follow them carefully, one at a time. If you are not sure what to do, ask an adult.

Experiment symbols

① Shows how long the experiment will take, once you have collected all the equipment you need.

② Shows if you need to ask an adult to help you with the experiment.

③ Shows how easy or difficult the experiment is to do.

Introduction
See what you will be learning about in each experiment.

Things you will need
You should be able to find the equipment around the house or at a supermarket. No special equipment is needed. Always ask before using materials from home.

Safety
If there is a "Help needed" symbol at the start of the experiment, you must ask an adult to help you.

The warning symbol also tells you to be careful when using knives or scissors, or heat. Always ask an adult for help.

SALTY to freshwater

Can you separate the salt and water in salty water? Yes, by distillation – try this experiment to see how.

① 30 min ② Help needed ③ Tricky

You will need
- work surface
- stovetop
- water
- glass
- table salt
- teaspoon
- small dish
- saucepan
- aluminum foil
- ice cubes
- jug

(a) Half fill a glass with water. Add four teaspoons of salt and stir to make the salt dissolve. This is the salty solution.

(b) Pour most of the salty water into a saucepan. Then stand a small dish in the center. *There should be no water in this dish*

(c) Put a piece of aluminum foil over the top of the pan. Gently press down the center slightly to make a dip. Put a few ice cubes in the dip.

Stages
Numbers and letters guide you through the stages of each experiment.

Doing the experiments

✹ Clear a surface to work on, such as a table, and cover it with newspaper if you need to.

✹ You could wear an apron or an old T-shirt to protect your clothing.

✹ Gather all the equipment you need before you start, and tidy up after each experiment.

✹ Ask an adult to help you when an experiment is marked with a "Help needed" or warning symbol.

✹ Work over a tray or sink when you are pouring water.

✹ Always ask an adult to help you if you are unsure what to do.

Put the pan on the stovetop and heat it gently. Allow the water to boil for a few minutes (but make sure all the solution does not boil away). Be careful, as the water will get hot.

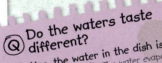

Explanation
At the end of each experiment is a question-and-answer explanation. It tells you what should have happened and why.

Q Do the waters taste different?

A Yes, the water in the dish is freshwater – free of salt. The water evaporated (turned to steam), leaving the salt behind in the pan, but the steam condensed (turned to water) on the cold foil and the water dripped into the dish. This process is called distillation and it is used to get freshwater from seawater.

Make sure the dish is cold before you touch it

Remove the saucepan from the stovetop and leave it for 1 hour to cool completely. Then remove the foil. There should now be water in the dish. Taste the water in the pan and the water in the dish.

Also try... In the experiment on distillation, you removed the salt from the water and kept the water.

If you just want to keep the salt, put a saucer of the salty water in a warm place. The water will slowly evaporate, leaving the salt behind.

Also try...
Simple mini experiments test the science you've learned.

Labels
Handy labels will provide you with useful tips and information to help your experiment run smoothly.

Scientist KIT

Before you begin experimenting you will need to gather some equipment. You should be able to find all of it around the house or at a local supermarket. Ask an adult's permission before using anything and take care when you see a warning sign.

From the craft box

- colored pencils
- felt-tip pens (water soluble)
- lead pencils
- pencil sharpener
- tape
- thick card stock
- thin card stock

From the Kitchen

- cutting board
- colander
- funnel
- glasses
- jars
- jug
- Aluminum foil
- Paper towels
- knife
- saucepan with lid
- saucers
- scissors
- sieve
- small dish
- tablespoons
- teaspoons
- thermometer
- bowl
- wooden spoon

Handy hint!
Ice cubes and frozen peas will melt very quickly. Leave them in the freezer until you are ready to use them.

Foody things

- baking soda
- cooking oil
- flour
- food coloring
- ice cubes
- lemon juice
- milk
- peas
- red cabbage
- table salt
- tea bag
- vinegar
- water

 Warning!
Scissors and knives are sharp and can cut you easily. Make sure you ask an adult for help. When passing scissors or a knife, point the blunt end towards the other person.

Other stuff

- 9V battery
- balloon
- Epsom salts
- filter paper
- household bleach
- petroleum jelly
- short sticks
- small plastic drink bottle

Warning!
Bleach can be dangerous if not used correctly. Ask an adult for help and if you get any on your skin, wash it off immediately with water.

Petroleum jelly

Places you'll need to work
- fridge
- stovetop
- oven
- work surface

Balloons

Warning!
Be careful not to burn yourself on the stovetop. Remember it is hot enough to cook food on! Ask an adult for help.

Remember to recycle and reuse

One way to help the environment is by recycling and reusing materials such as glass, paper, plastics, and scrap metals. It is mostly cheaper and less wasteful than making new products from stratch.

Reusing means you use materials again in their original form rather than throwing them away.

Recycling is when materials are taken to a plant where they can be melted and remade into either the same or new products.

Peas

Handy hint!
Plastic bottles come in many different colors. Try to use a clear bottle so that you can see your experiment working.

11

ICE TO water to steam

Ice, liquid water, and steam are just water, but in solid, liquid, and gas forms. Solids, liquids, and gases are the three states of matter. This experiment shows that water has different properties in each of the three states.

15 min | Help needed | Easy

You will need
- stovetop
- saucepan with lid
- wooden spoon
- ice cubes
- thermometer that measures from 32°F to 212°F

Gently heat the saucepan and stir the ice. Ask an adult to help you heat the water because the stovetop will become hot. When the ice has begun to melt, test the temperature of the water with the thermometer.

Put a saucepan on the stovetop, covering the bottom of it with ice cubes. Press on the ice cubes with the wooden spoon and watch what happens.

Q Does the ice flow?

A No, at first the solid ice doesn't flow or change shape. As the temperature of the water rises, it changes state – from solid ice to liquid water. This change from solid to liquid is called melting, and for ice, it normally happens at 32°F.

12

Keep heating and melting the ice until you have liquid water. Look at how the liquid is different than the solid.

Extreme steam!

Soon you will see bubbles forming – the liquid water is turning to steam. Put a lid on the pan and turn off the heat before all the water is gone. You should have a pan full of steam. Don't touch the pan, as the steam will be very hot.

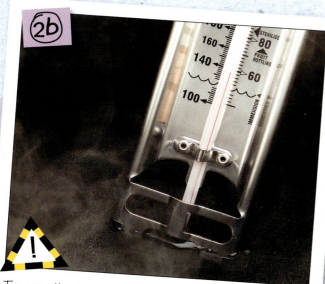

Turn up the heat. Ask an adult to help you test the temperature again to see if it has changed.

Q Does the water flow?
A Yes, the liquid water flows. It changes shape and flows to fill the bottom of the saucepan.

Q What does the steam do?
A The steam fills the saucepan. If you were to remove the lid, it would escape. The liquid water has changed to steam. This change of state is called boiling. For water, it normally happens at 212°F.

CREATE crystals

Have you ever looked really closely at table salt or sugar? If so, you've already seen crystals. Here's how to grow some crystals of your own.

 15 min preparation, 3 days for results
 Help needed
 Hard

You will need
- work surface
- oven
- fridge
- table salt
- Epsom salts
- 2 glasses
- jug
- 2 teaspoons
- 4 saucers
- water
- optional: food coloring

Preparation

Half fill two glasses with warm water. Add a few teaspoons of table salt to one glass and a few teaspoons of Epsom salts to the other glass. Stir the water in each glass so that the salts dissolve. These are your salt solutions. You could add a few drops of food coloring for fun.

1a

Don't add too much solution to the water

Pour a little table salt solution onto two saucers. Leave one saucer in a warm place. Examine the crystals after one hour, then at regular intervals for about three days.

1b

Ask an adult to put the other saucer in the oven at 275°F/140°C for about 15 minutes or until all the water has evaporated. Carefully remove the crystals from the oven and examine them.

Q What shape are the crystals?
A The table salt crystals look like cubes.
They are called cubic crystals. In the solution you made, the tiny particles of table salt were mixed with water. As the water evaporated in the air or oven, the particles joined together to make crystals. Crystals have straight edges and flat faces because the particles are arranged in a neat, regular way.

Crystals formed in a warm place
After 3 days

Crystals formed in the oven
After 15 minutes

 2a
Pour some Epsom salt solution onto two saucers. Put one saucer in a warm place and examine the crystals at regular intervals for a few days.

2b
Put the other saucer in the fridge. Examine the crystals after 10 minutes, 30 minutes, and 1 hour.

Q Are the Epsom salt crystals different?
A Yes, the Epsom salt crystals are needle shaped. Just like the cubic crystals, they have straight edges and flat faces.

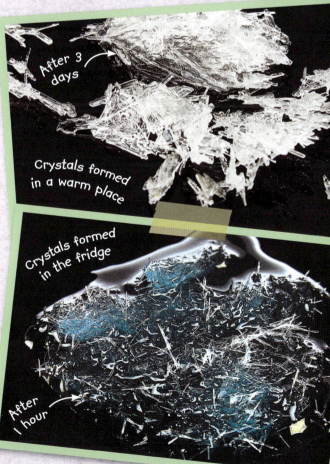

After 3 days
Crystals formed in a warm place

Crystals formed in the fridge
After 1 hour

15

Mixing like MAGIC

Materials are made of millions of tiny particles. This experiment shows that in a liquid, the particles are constantly jiggling and moving.

15 min preparation, 30 min for results — Help needed — Tricky

You will need
- work surface
- petroleum jelly
- 2 clean, empty jars
- food coloring
- water
- spoon
- jug
- piece of thin card stock
- bowl

a

Make the jelly really thick

Smear plenty of petroleum jelly around the rims of the two jars to make a watertight seal.

c

Fill the other jar with water, right to the top, too.

b

Half fill one of the jars with water, add a few drops of food coloring, and stir. Then fill the jar with water, right to the brim.

d

Make the card stock 1 inch bigger than the jar

Cut a square of thin card stock, large enough to cover the opening of one of the jars. Put it on top of the jar with colored water in it.

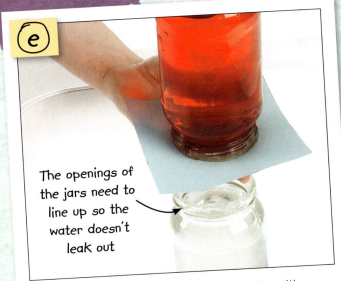

The openings of the jars need to line up so the water doesn't leak out

Place the jar of clear water in the bowl. With one hand supporting the card stock, carefully turn over the jar of colored water. Slowly slip out your hand and place the top jar on the bottom jar. You might need some help with this. Leave the jars to settle for 10 minutes before moving on to step f.

While holding the top jar steady, slowly and carefully slide out the card stock. Again, you might need some help with this step.

Dark red... lighter... light red!

Clear... darker... light red!

After 1 minute | After 10 minutes | After 30 minutes

Q: What happens to the colored water?

A: It mixes with the clear water. The tiny water molecules are tightly packed together and are constantly moving. The water molecules from the two jars slowly mix together, carrying the particles of food coloring with them.

17

Can you MIX IT?

Many materials are made by mixing other materials. In these experiments, you'll put two different materials in the same container to see that some mix well and others don't mix at all.

 15 min   No help needed   Easy

You will need
- work surface
- 5 jars
- cooking oil
- water
- 5 spoons
- table salt
- flour

1

Put some water and cooking oil into a jar and stir with a spoon.

2

Add salt

Half fill a clean jar with water, add a spoonful of salt, and stir.

Q Do oil and water mix?

A No matter how much you stir, the oil and water don't mix. After stirring, they quickly separate again, leaving a layer of oil on top of the water. This is because the particles of oil and the particles of water repel each other.

Q Do salt and water mix?

A Yes, when you mix salt with water, the salt seems to disappear. In fact, it dissolves – it breaks into tiny particles that mix with the water. The mixture is called a solution.

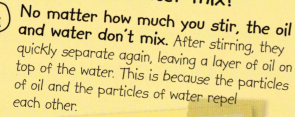

18

③

Use a clean jar and mix a spoonful of flour into half a jar of water.

Q Do flour and water mix?

A Yes, flour and water mix. Unlike oil and water, flour mixes much better and forms a paste. This is because the water and flour do not repel each other.

Goooey!

⑤

Add as much salt as possible

Half fill a clean jar with water, add five spoonfuls of salt, and stir. Add another five spoonfuls and keep stirring.

④

Pour some cooking oil into a clean jar. Add a few pinches of salt to the oil and stir.

Q How much salt will dissolve?

A Lots! Eventually you will not be able to make any more salt disappear into the water. There are no water particles free to break up any more salt.

Q Do oil and salt mix?

A No, the salt does not dissolve. Instead it just sinks to the bottom. This is because the oil does not break up the salt crystals like water does.

Leftover salt

19

SPLITTING the mix

A mixture is made up of two or more different materials mixed together. Sometimes you may want to separate the materials in a mixture.

30 min | No help needed | Hard

You will need
- work surface
- 3 clean, empty jars
- water
- teaspoon
- tea bag
- table salt
- peas (frozen or fresh, not canned)
- colander
- bowl
- paper towels or filter paper

Preparation

Half fill three jars with water. Add some frozen or fresh peas to the first jar. Add the tea leaves from a tea bag to the second jar. Stir two teaspoons of salt into the third jar.

①

Place a colander over a bowl. Pour half the mixture of water and peas into the colander.

Q Can you separate the peas?

A Yes, you can. The colander's holes are small enough to trap the peas.

Pour half the mixture of tea leaves and water through the colander, and then half the mixture of salt and water.

Put a paper towel in the colander. Pour the rest of the the tea and water mixture through.

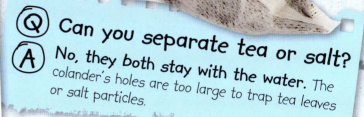

Q: Can you separate tea or salt?
A: No, they both stay with the water. The colander's holes are too large to trap tea leaves or salt particles.

Use a clean paper towel

Put a new paper towel in the colander. Pour the rest of the salt and water mixture through the paper. Dip your finger in the water and taste it.

Q: Does a filter stop the tea leaves?
A: Yes, it does. The paper towel has very small holes between the paper fibers. They are small enough to trap the tea leaves, but not the water.

Q: Can you filter salt from water?
A: No, the filter paper lets salt water through. This is why the water tastes salty. The particles of salt water are extremely tiny and easily pass through the holes.

SALTY to freshwater

Can you separate the salt and water in salty water? Yes, by distillation – try this experiment to see how.

30 min | Help needed | Tricky

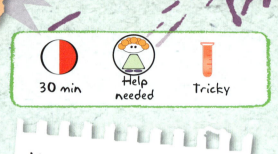

You will need
- work surface
- stovetop
- water
- glass
- table salt
- teaspoon
- small dish
- saucepan
- aluminum foil
- ice cubes
- jug

a Half fill a glass with water. Add four teaspoons of salt and stir to make the salt dissolve. This is the salty solution.

b Pour most of the salty water into a saucepan. Then stand a small dish in the center.

There should be no water in this dish

c Put a piece of aluminum foil over the top of the pan. Gently press down the center slightly to make a dip. Put a few ice cubes in the dip.

d Put the pan on the stovetop and heat it gently. Allow the water to boil for a few minutes (but make sure all the solution does not boil away). Be careful, as the water will get hot.

Make sure the dish is cold before you touch it

e Remove the saucepan from the stovetop and leave it for 1 hour to cool completely. Then remove the foil. There should now be water in the dish. Taste the water in the pan and the water in the dish.

Q Do the waters taste different?

A **Yes, the water in the dish is freshwater – free of salt.** The water evaporated (turned to steam), leaving the salt behind in the pan, but the steam condensed (turned to water) on the cold foil and the water dripped into the dish. This process is called distillation and it is used to get freshwater from seawater.

Also try... In the experiment on distillation, you removed the salt from the water and kept the water.

If you just want to keep the salt, put a saucer of the salty water in a warm place. The water will slowly evaporate, leaving the salt behind.

COLOR separation

Inks, food coloring, and dyes are often mixtures containing different colors called pigments. Try this experiment to separate pigments so that you can see what they are.

 30 min No help needed Hard

You will need
- work surface
- 4 strips of filter paper, 1 in by 4 in
- water
- 4 clean, empty jars
- 4 pencils or short sticks
- tape
- 4 water-soluble felt-tip pens or food coloring
- scissors
- water
- jug

(a) Wrap a strip of filter paper around each of your four pencils, so the paper is as long as your jar is tall. Stick it to the pencil with tape.

(b) Put about 1 inch of water in each of the four jars.

Trim any excess paper

> **Q** What happens to the dots?
>
> **A** The colors spread out and separate.
> The filter paper strips soak up the water. The water picks up the different pigments in the ink and carries them upwards through the paper. The water on the paper slowly evaporates, and this draws more water upwards. Different pigments are carried different distances up the paper, and thus are separated.

Use plenty of food coloring or ink

About 1 inch from the end of each strip, either draw a large dot with a felt-tip pen or add a drop of food coloring.

After 10 minutes

green = yellow + blue

After 30 minutes

yellow – no change

blue = red + blue

Carefully lower a strip (with the colored dot at the bottom end) into each jar, so the dot is about one centimeter above the water's surface. Examine the paper every ten minutes for an hour.

red = yellow + purple

After 1 hour

25

CABBAGE colors

What links lemon juice and bleach? One is an acid and the other is an alkali. They are opposites. Here's an experiment to show what is acid and what is alkali – using cabbage!

 30 min   Help needed   Tricky

You will need
- work surface
- stovetop
- red cabbage
- knife
- cutting board
- saucepan
- sieve
- 3 clean, empty jars
- bowl
- teaspoons
- lemon juice
- baking soda
- household bleach
- water

Preparation

(a) Ask an adult to chop half a red cabbage into small pieces.

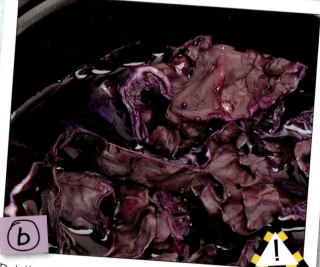

(b) Put the pieces of cabbage in a saucepan and cover with water. Ask an adult to bring it to a boil and simmer for five minutes. Turn off the heat and allow the water and cabbage to cool.

(c) Hold a sieve over the bowl. Pour the cabbage and water through it, so the purple water collects in the bowl.

(d) Half fill the three jars with some of the purple water. The purple color means the liquid is neutral.

① Add a few drops of bleach to the first jar and stir. Ask an adult to help you pour the bleach.

② Put a teaspoon of baking soda into the third jar and stir.

Q What does bleach do to the water?
A It turns the purple water green, then yellow. Bleach is an alkali.

Q What does baking soda do to the water?
A It turns the purple color to blue. Baking soda is a chemical called a base, which turns water into an alkali. But it is not as alkaline as the bleach.

③ Put a few drops of lemon juice into the second jar and stir.

Bleach — Strong alkali
Lemon juice — Acid
Baking soda — Weak alkali

Q What does lemon juice do to the water?
A Lemon juice turns the water red. It is an acid.

By changing color, the cabbage water tells us whether chemicals are acids or alkalis. It is called an indicator.

27

Bubbles AND FROTH

A chemical reaction is when materials are changed into new materials. Here's your chance to see chemical reactions at work.

 30 min   No help needed   Easy

You will need
- work surface
- milk
- 2 glasses
- tablespoons
- vinegar
- filter paper
- funnel
- baking soda
- small plastic drink bottle
- balloon
- saucer

1a

Put half a cup of milk into a glass and stir in two tablespoons of vinegar. The vinegar will make the milk turn lumpy.

1b

Stinky, ewwwww!

Strain the mixture through filter paper into another glass. You don't need to keep the liquid.

1c

After an hour or two, remove the pasty substance from the paper onto a saucer.

Q: What do vinegar and milk make?

A: They make a pasty substance. A material called casein in the milk reacts with the vinegar to make a new substance, which turns hard like plastic when it dries.

Touch it, if you dare!

Put the narrow part of a funnel into the neck of a balloon. Carefully put two tablespoons of baking soda into the funnel and shake it down into the balloon.

Up, up and away!

Don't tip any baking soda into the bottle yet

Add 1 inch of vinegar to the bottle. Then carefully attach the balloon to the top of the bottle.

Lift up the balloon and shake it so the baking soda falls into the bottle.

Q What happens to the balloon?
A **The balloon inflates!** The vinegar reacts with the baking soda, making carbon dioxide gas. This gas fills the balloon.

29

ELECTRIC bubble maker

In this experiment you send electricity through water. The electricity breaks up the water, making tiny bubbles of gas.

30 min — No help needed — Hard

You will need
- work surface
- thick card stock
- clean, empty jar
- 2 lead pencils, the same length
- pencil sharpener
- water
- 9V battery

a Cut a square of thick card stock about 1 inch wider than the opening of the jar.

b Sharpen both ends of the pencils. Then carefully push the pencils through the card stock, about 1 inch apart.

c Half fill the jar with water. Then place the card stock on top of the jar and slide the pencils up or down so that their ends are level and underwater.

Don't let the pencils touch the bottom

(d)

Hold the battery upside down on top of the pencils so that the battery terminals touch the pencil leads.

Also try...

Add some salt to the water, stir it in, and repeat the experiment. Sniff the air above the jar. Can you smell chlorine or a "swimming pool" smell? When you add salt, chlorine comes from the pencil lead attached to the positive terminal. Chlorine is one of the elements in salt (which is sodium chloride, or NaCl).

pop! pop! pop!
bubbly

Q Can you see bubbles?

A The small bubbles that appear on the pencil leads and rise to the surface are **bubbles of oxygen and hydrogen**. These are the two chemical elements in water. Oxygen is produced when the pencil lead touches the positive battery terminal, and hydrogen is made when the pencil lead touches the negative battery terminal.

GLOSSARY

Acid A chemical substance that has a pH level of less than 7.
Alkali A chemical substance that has a pH level of more than 7.
Atom The smallest particle of an element.
Boiling point The temperature at which a liquid bubbles and changes into a gas when it is heated.
Condensing The process of a gas changing to a liquid as it cools.
Dissolving If a solid dissolves, it mixes with a liquid and makes a solution.
Distillation The process used to separate a liquid from a solution by evaporation and condensing.
Element A simple chemical substance that consists of only one kind of atom, and cannot be broken down.
Evaporation The process in which water is heated and changes from a liquid to a gas.
Filter To separate two substances in a mixture by passing it through something, such as a sieve.
Freezing point The temperature at which a liquid cools and changes into a solid.
Material What every substance is made from. Materials can be natural (e.g. wood) or synthetic (e.g. polyester).
Matter All substances are made up of very small particles, or matter, and can be a solid, liquid, or gas.

Melting The process that changes a solid into a liquid, mainly when heated.
Mixture A substance that contains two or more different substances that are mixed, but not chemically bound. They can be easily separated.
Molecule At least two atoms held together by a chemical bond.
Neutral A chemical substance with a pH level equal to 7.
Pigment A mixture of different colors that make up one color when put together.
Reaction When a chemical change occurs and materials are changed into new materials. For example, when vinegar reacts with baking soda, carbon dioxide is made.
Repel When two or more substances do not mix.
Separation When two or more materials in a mixture are moved apart.
Solution A mixture in which a gas, solid, or liquid is dissolved in a liquid.
Thermometer A piece of equipment used to measure temperature.

INDEX

A
acids 26–27
alkalis 26–27
atoms 6
B
boiling 13, 23, 26
C
carbon dioxide 29
chemical reactions 28
chlorine 31
color 4, 7, 10–11, 24–27
condensing 6, 23
cotton 7
crystals 4, 14–15, 19
D
dissolving 14, 18–19, 22
distillation 22–23

E
electricity 30
elements 31
evaporation 6, 14–15, 23, 25
F
filters 11, 20–21, 24–25, 28
freezing 6
G
gases 6, 12, 29–30
H
hydrogen 31
I
ice 10, 12–13, 22
L
liquids 6, 12–13, 16, 26, 28

M
materials 4–5, 7–8, 11, 16, 18, 20, 28
melting 6, 12–13
mixtures 7, 18, 20–21, 24, 28
molecules 6, 17
N
natural materials 7
O
oxygen 31
P
petroleum 7, 11, 16
pigments 24–25
plastic 7, 11, 28
polyester 7

R
recycling 11
reusing materials 11
rubber 7
S
separation 18, 20–22, 24–25
solids 6, 12, 13
solutions 14–15, 18, 22–23
states of matter 6, 12
steam 12–13, 23
synthetic materials 7
W
wood 7, 10, 12